YOUR KNOWLEDGE HAS VALUE

Bibliographic information published by the German National Library:

The German National Library lists this publication in the National Bibliography; detailed bibliographic data are available on the Internet at http://dnb.dnb.de .

Imprint:

Copyright © 2016 GRIN Verlag, Open Publishing GmbH
Print and binding: Books on Demand GmbH, Norderstedt Germany
ISBN: 9783668215924

This book at GRIN:

http://www.grin.com/en/e-book/321036/using-different-assessment-screens-to-evaluate-students-object-oriented

Yeeshtdevisingh Hosanee

Using different assessment screens to evaluate students' Object-Oriented Programming (OOP) skills

GRIN Publishing

GRIN - Your knowledge has value

Since its foundation in 1998, GRIN has specialized in publishing academic texts by students, college teachers and other academics as e-book and printed book. The website www.grin.com is an ideal platform for presenting term papers, final papers, scientific essays, dissertations and specialist books.

Visit us on the internet:

http://www.grin.com/

http://www.facebook.com/grincom

http://www.twitter.com/grin_com

Different assessment screens to evaluate Object-Oriented Programming (OOP) students

Yeeshtdevisingh Hosanee

Abstract

Assessing students in classrooms is important. Self-assessment is also another important part in teaching and learning. It helps both teachers and the students to understand where to improve in the school curriculum. Therefore in this paper we have talked on the different self-assessment screens which are available to teach computer programming. We proposed a new way of self-assessing novice learners to evaluate novice Object-Oriented Programming (OOP) learners theoretical and java coding skills. A previous work was published (Hosanee, 2015) where the requirements of a novice OOP tool were identified. An OOP novice learning tool was built. The software consisted of many features. E-assessment was among one of the software. Therefore, in this paper, the assessments screens are being evaluated. Feedbacks received from novice OOP learners confirmed that the screens were simple and students enjoyed answering the questions.

Keywords:
Object-Oriented Programming(OOP), novice OOP learners, software tool, assessment tools, inheritance OOP concept, association OOP concept, formative assessment, summative assessment, sub-classes and super classes.

1.   Introduction

Assessment is an important factor to evaluate the performance of a student (Shepard, 2000). Everywhere around the world, we perform different classroom assessments at the different educational level: primary secondary and tertiary. Even at job interviews, we perform different assessments (monstertrak.com, 2001; M, 2009). This is a reflection of the skills and knowledge that one possesses. To successfully pass an assessment, self-assessment can help to achieve this. We usually self-assess ourselves before going to an exam or for a job interview. Therefore, both types of assessment, the classroom assessment and the self-assessment, are important to an individual (gov.on.ca, 2007; A.Ross, 2006; Desjarlais & Smith, 2011). Classroom assessment is a formal one and a self-assessment is an informal one (Jeff, 2013; Roder, 2004).

Today, there exist few researches (KHAMIS et al., 2008) being carried out to assess computer programming student's skills although much work is being done to improve existing software and teaching skills to allow maximum students to engage themselves when they are learning computer programming. Existing self-assessment evaluation screens evaluate the students' coding skills only, but not his/her theoretical knowledge. Therefore, in this paper, we present different optional screens where we can have both theoretical and coding questions in the same software for the students to understand OOP properly.

2.   Background study

One of the biggest challenges of teachers is to how to evaluate students' programming skills (Bennedsen & Carpersen, 2006). The main issues with teaching OOP to students are the lack of teachers to teach and the lack of quality instructional materials (Kellaghan & Greaney, 2001). Therefore, we are not able to assess these students properly as they are not supported correctly to learn OOP concepts. Hence, self-learning becomes important when teachers are not able to provide the support needed (Kemppainen & Hein, 2008).

As already mentioned in the introduction section, today we have many undergoing researches for teaching OOP, but we have few researches regarding the evaluation of the skills of OOP learners (KHAMIS et al., 2008). Assessment can be in two categories   (KHAMIS et al., 2008): formative assessment and summative assessment. Formative assessment is an assessment which occurs at the start of the program or during the usage of the program. It provides an immediate feedback to the student on the particular feature he is working with. Formative assessment allows teachers and "students with information and insights needed to improve teaching effectiveness and learning quality". On the other hand, summative assessment is carried out at the end of a program. It is used to check the level of learning. It is usually the final grade of the student. Therefore, undergoing researches include both formative assessment and summative assessment   (KHAMIS et al., 2008) effectiveness. Typical examples of these researches include the evaluation of OOP skills based on their emotional state (Martin, 2012), designing a new approach with the Delphi technique to evaluate OOP learners' skills (KHAMIS et al., 2008), designing a criterion-referenced assessment model which is derived from Goal Questions Metrics methodology (Khamis et al., 2007), on self-assessment of OOP (Antala & Koncz, 2011) , the outside-in methods (Janke & Wagner, 2015) , using a User Knowledge Assessment Tool (UKAT) to "personalise training and facilitate self-learning" (Seffah et al., 1999), self-assessment of OOP skills via the web known as quizzjet (Hsiao et al., 2008), a platform to self-evaluate students' java programming skills (Bettini et al., 2004).

3.   Methodology

The Methodology consists of integrating both summative and formative self-assessment questions for students to self-learn OOP in OOP novice software learning tool. Both theoretical and coding skills should be assessed. Most questions in self-assessment screens should be related to what has been taught previously during the class session. In this paper, we choose java programming language for the coding assessments. An evaluation with some students has been done to assess the different self-assessment screens in the OOP novice tool built.

4.   Results

A prior work (Hosanee, 2015) was conducted to determine the requirements of OOP novice learners. Based on these data, a software with assessments screens were built. In this paper, we will show the results of the self-assessment screens only. In the first part of this section, we will show you the screens for OOP theoretical questions and in the second part of this section, we will show you the different java coding assessment screens which were built. Questions in both parts are typical examples of inheritance and association, two of the many concepts of OOP.

4.1. Theoretical self-assessments questions

4.1.a. First Method

The following figure shows a self-assessment screens which allow OOP learners to evaluate their basic OOP concepts. Questions are in fill-in the blank type. For instance, the user is expected to select the appropriate answer from the different combo boxes in every sentences. He will be expected to click on the "validate" button to validate his answers. If he fails to answer to the questions, he will be prompted to try again until he is able to answer all the questions successfully. Feedbacks received for this screens confirm that the screen is simple and fun. Students enjoy the fill-in the blank features.

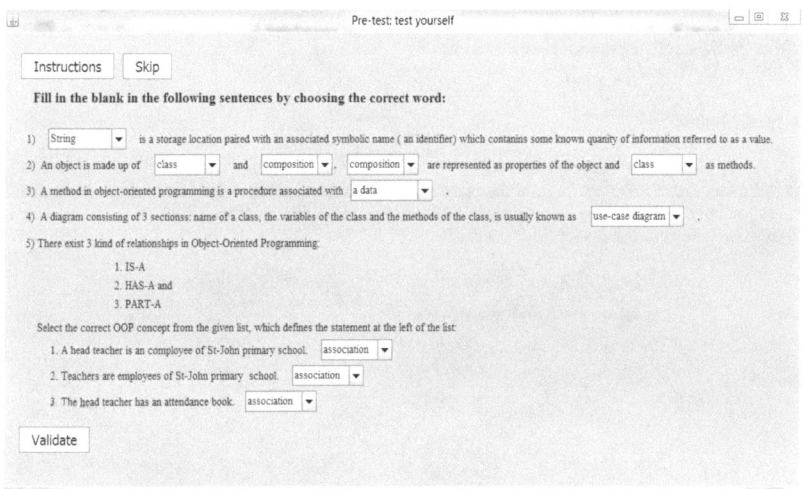

Figure 1 Fill-in the blank question

4.1.b. Second Method

Formative and summative questions can be as in the next figure as well. To teach inheritance (one of the concepts of OOP), three classes were used. "Person", "Staff" and "Student". Staff and student classes inherited their characteristics from the class person. Therefore, Person is known to be the parent of children staff and Student. Therefore, we designed the questions accordingly to allow the novice learner to define the relationship between Person, Staff and Student. Feedbacks received were positive. Learners have been able to identify the relationships between the 3 classes. They have understood that staff and students are subclasses of class Person.

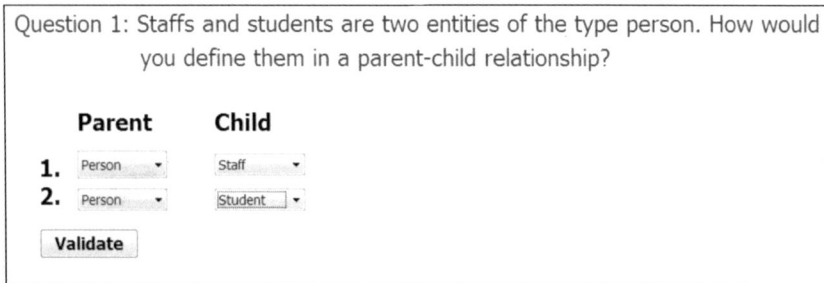

Figure 2 Inheritance theoretical question

4.2. Java coding self-assessments questions

4.2.a. First Method

In the following figure, we show one of the many ways to test the coding skills of a student. We can ask the latter a theoretical question based on what he can visualize. For instance, in the figure, the user is asked to identify the constructor of the class staff.

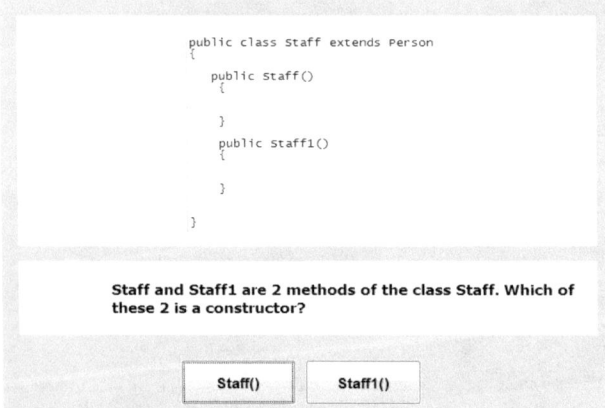

Figure 3 Java coding theoretical question (a)

When the user fails to answer question, a message with "incorrect answer" is displayed on the screen.

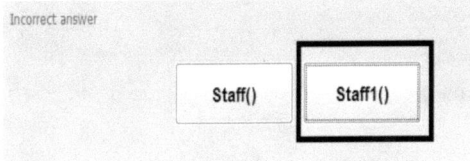

Figure 4 Java coding theoretical question (b)

When the user answers the question successfully, he/she is allowed to move to the next question:

Figure 5 Java coding theoretical question (c)

Feedback received for this particular type of assessment question was again positive. Novice learners enjoy the 2 button options features. If they fail to answer a question correctly, they immediately understand the right answer as they have only two possibilities. They also find the screens easy and simple. They have been able to acquire OOP concepts both theoretically (understand the OOP technical words and architecture) and technically (by understanding the java codes).

4.2.b. Second Method

Another way to test student's java coding skills is to ask the user different questions and he is expected to type in the answers. Feedbacks received for all the java coding assessments screens were encouraging. Students were able to understand OOP concepts consistently. Again, the simplicity of the screens was appealing to the students. It motivated them to use the software and to learn OOP.

4.2.b.1. Inheritance Java question:

In the following diagram, there exist three text area boxes to define relationships between subclasses and their super classes to understand inheritance (one of OOP concepts). The user is expected to answer in the appropriate text area box/boxes and validate his/her answer by clicking on the "Next" button.

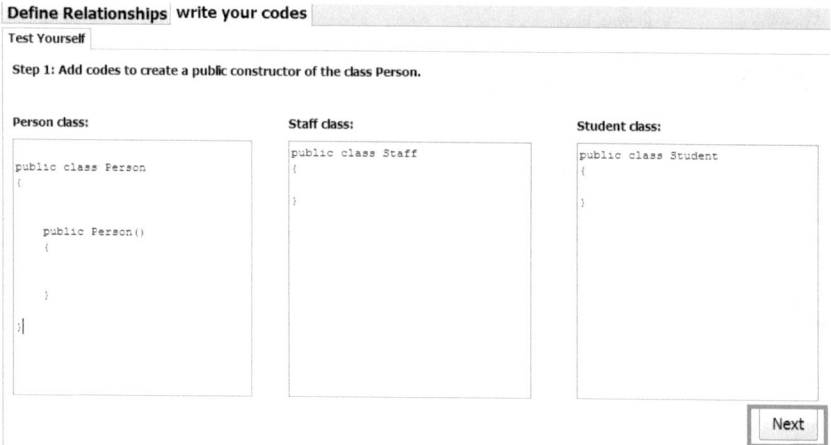

Figure 6 Java coding inheritance question

4.2.b.2. Association Java question:

Another example where a user is expected to type in the correct answer in text boxes is shown below. This screen was designed to test the user's proficiency level on "association" (One of OOP concepts). If the user answers correctly, he will be informed on the screen "correct answer!"

Question:

Given the codes for the class Person, staff , student and Pen , add the code which will allow any staffs or any students can use a pen.

Perform an association where any staff or student is able to use a public class variable "pen_object" of type Pen. The variable should be initialised to a null value. (Please, write the additional codes on the first line of the class)

Correct answer! You may close this window.

Person, staff and Student classes:

```
public class Person
{
    public Pen pen_object = null;

    public int current_year = 2015;
    public String first_name = "";

    public Person()
    {

    }
    public void set_name(String name)
```

Pen class:

```
public Pen()
{

}

public String get_size()
{

    return "HB";
}
```

Figure 7 Association java coding question (1)

6

The following diagram shows the screen when a user fails to answer the question:

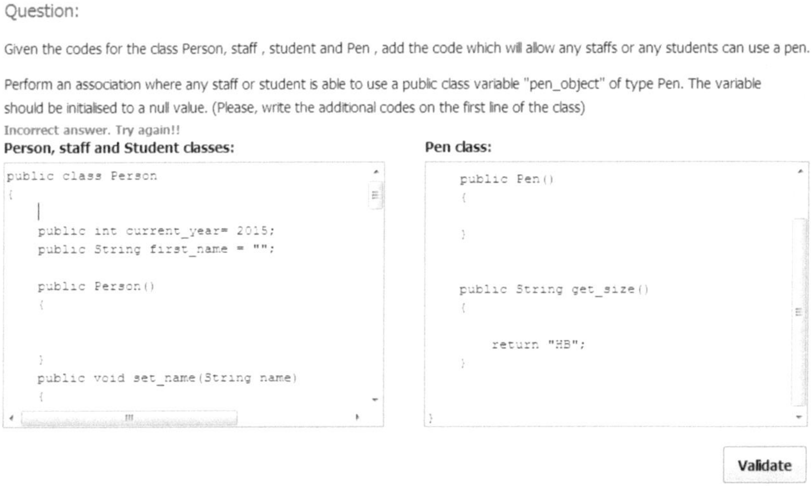

Question:

Given the codes for the class Person, staff , student and Pen , add the code which will allow any staffs or any students can use a pen.

Perform an association where any staff or student is able to use a public class variable "pen_object" of type Pen. The variable should be initialised to a null value. (Please, write the additional codes on the first line of the class)

Incorrect answer. Try again!!

Person, staff and Student classes:

```
public class Person
{
    |

    public int current_year= 2015;
    public String first_name = "";

    public Person()
    {


    }
    public void set_name(String name)
    {
```

Pen class:

```
public Pen()
{

}

public String get_size()
{

    return "HB";
}
```

Validate

Figure 8 Association java coding question (2)

5.   Conclusion

Both formal assessments and self-assessments are important to students   (jiscinfonet, n.d.). They both help students to evaluate themselves effectively. The different assessments screens can be used either as formal assessment or self-assessment. As we can see, the results were positive. Students were able to grasp OOP concepts with more fun than before. They were more motivated to learn with the simplicity of the screens.

For a future work, we should be able to perform the evaluation in a larger scale with more than hundred users. In this way, we will be able to develop an assessment learning culture (SHEPAR, 2000) because assessment is perceived as the bridge between teaching and learning (SHEPAR, 2000).

References

A.Ross, J., 2006. The Reliability, Validity, and Utility of self-assessment. *Practical Assessment Research and Evaluation*, 11(10).

Antala, M. & Koncz, S., 2011. Learning behaviors measured by a web-based self-assessment system. *Journal of educational sciences and psychology*, 1(1), pp.51-56.

Bennedsen, J. & Carpersen, E.M., 2006. A Competence Model for Object Interaction in Introductory Programming. In *in Proceeding of 18th Workshop of the Psychology of Programming Interest Group.*, 2006.

Bettini, L. et al., 2004. An Environment for Self-Assessing Java Programming Skills in Undergraduate First Programming Courses. *ICALT 2004,Joensuu, Finland.*

Desjarlais, M. & Smith, P., 2011. *A Comparative Analysis of Reflection and Self-Assessment.* http://www.processeducation.org/ijpe/2011/reflection.pdf.

gov.on.ca, 2007. *Student self-assessment.* http://www.edu.gov.on.ca/eng/literacynumeracy/inspire/research/studentselfassessment.pdf.

Hosanee, Y. &. P. S., 2015. *An enhanced software tool to aid novices in learning Object Oriented Programming (OOP).* In *Proceedings of Computing, Communication and Security (ICCCS), 2015 International Conference* on IEEExplore.

Hsiao, I.H., Brusilovsky, P. & Sosnovsky, S., 2008. Web-based Parameterized Questions for Object-Oriented Programming. In *Proceedings of E-Learn: World Conference on E-Learning in Corporate, Government, Healthcare, and Higher Education.*, 2008.

Iskander, M., 2008. *Innovative Techniques in Instruction Technology, E-learning.*

Janke, E. & Wagner, s., 2015. Does Outside-In Teaching Improve the Learning of Object-Oriented Programming? Available at: https://www.hs-neu-ulm.de/fileadmin/user_upload/Forschung/Forschungsprojekte/EVELIN/PID3563647.pdf.

Jeff, 2013. *Informal vs. Formal Assessments: Tests are not the only end-all-be-all of how we assess.* [Online] Available at: https://jeffreymdelacruz.wordpress.com/2013/02/20/informal-vs-formal-assessments-tests-are-not-the-only-end-all-be-all-of-how-we-assess/ [Accessed 08 April 2016].

jiscinfonet, n.d. *Effective Use of VLEs:e−Assessment.* http://tools.jiscinfonet.ac.uk/downloads/vle/eassessment-printable.pdf.

Kellaghan, T. & Greaney, v., 2001. *using assessment to improve qualtiy of education.* http://unesdoc.unesco.org/images/0012/001262/126231e.pdf.

Kemppainen, A. & Hein, G., 2008. Enhancing Student Learning Through SelfAssessment. In *38th ASEE/IEEE Frontiers in Education Conference.*, 2008. http://fie-conference.org/fie2008/papers/1128.pdf.

Khamis, N., Idris, S. & Ahmad, R., 2007. Applying GQM Approach towards Development of Criterion-Referenced Assessment Model for OO Programming Courses. *International Journal of Computer, Electrical, Automation, Control and Information Engineering* , 1(8).

KHAMIS, N., IDRIS, S., AHMAD, R. & IDRIS, N., 2008. Assessing Object-oriented Programming Skills in the Core Education of Computer Science and Information Technology: Introducing New Possible Approach. *WSEAS TRANSACTIONS on COMPUTERS* , 7(9).

M, T., 2009. The employment interview: A review of current studies and directions for future research. *Elsevier - Human Resource Management Review 19*, pp.203-18.

Martin, V.M.A., 2012. Evaluation of Object Oriented Programming Skills of Students with respect to Trait Emotional Intelligence based on Students Performance. *International Journal of Computer Applications (0975 – 888)*, 48(10).

monstertrak.com, 2001. *Preparing for interviews self-assessment and research.* https://www.dit.ie/media/careers/pdf/Preparing%20for%20interviews;%20self%20asssessment%20and%20research.pdf.

Rahmat, M., 2007. E-Learning Assessment Application Based on Bloom Taxonomy. *THE INTERNATIONAL JOURNAL OF LEARNING.*

Roder, N., 2004. *Self-assessment and informal learning within the professional framework of the operational Mobile Intensive Care paramedic.* https://minerva-access.unimelb.edu.au/handle/11343/57563.

Seffah, A., Bari, M. & Desmarais, M., 1999. Assessing Object-Oriented Technology Skills Using an Internet-Based System. *ACM.*

SHEPAR, L.A., 2000. The Role of Assessment in a Learning Culture. *Educational Researcher*, 29(7), pp.4-14.

Shepard, L.A., 2000. *The Role of Classroom Assessment in Teaching and Learning*. https://www.cse.ucla.edu/products/reports/TECH517.pdf.

Tea, T.B.b., 2013. Assessment: The Bridge between Teaching and Learning. *Voices from the Middle*, 21(2).

YOUR KNOWLEDGE HAS VALUE

- We will publish your bachelor's and
  master's thesis, essays and papers

- Your own eBook and book -
  sold worldwide in all relevant shops

- Earn money with each sale

Upload your text at www.GRIN.com
and publish for free